YOUR BRIDGE
to a
BETTER FUTURE

YOUR BRIDGE
— to a —
BETTER FUTURE

John C. Maxwell

Publishers Since 1798

THOMAS NELSON PUBLISHERS
Nashville • Atlanta • London • Vancouver

Published in Nashville, Tennessee, by Thomas Nelson, Inc., Publishers, and distributed in Canada by Word Communications, Ltd., Richmond, British Columbia.

The Scripture quotation in this publication is taken from *The Living Bible,* copyright 1971 by Tyndale House Publishers, Wheaton, IL. Used by permission.

ISBN 0-7852-7433-2

Printed in the United States of America.

1 2 3 4 5 6—02 01 00 99 98 97

Contents

Introduction

In *The Enormous Exception,* Earl Palmer
described the Golden Gate Bridge in this way:

It is built to sway some twenty feet at the
center of its one-mile suspension span. The
secret to its durability is its flexibility that
enables this sway, but that is not all. By
design, every part of the bridge—its concrete
roadway, its steel railings, its cross beams—is
inevitably related from one welded joint to
the other up through the vast cable system to
two great towers and two great land anchor
piers. The towers bear most of the weight,
and they are deeply imbedded into the rock
foundation beneath the sea. . . . This is its
secret! Flexibility and foundation.

Your bridge to a better future is a lot like the
Golden Gate Bridge in San Francisco. To stand
strong, it must be anchored to a solid foundation,
which gives it stability and longevity. But it must

also be flexible, to adapt to changing conditions—
and reach from where you are to where you're
going.

In life, each of us builds his or her own
bridge. The thoughts on the following pages are
there to help guide you through the process of
building the bridge that will carry you to a better
future.

John Maxwell
San Diego, California

YOUR DREAMS

Before you can proceed on any great journey, you must have a dream. The promise of the dream helps you take the first step. The hope of achieving the dream keeps you going, day after day, even when you feel too tired, sick, disappointed, or discouraged to take another step. The truth of the dream gives you strength to reach out and help others along the way. And the joy of fulfilling the dream and the promise of a better future lead to contentment. The journey ahead is awesome. But you can't get started until you've developed a dream.

"Vision is the world's most desperate need. There are no hopeless situations, only people who think hopelessly."

—Winifred Newman

■ *What would you say is the state of the world today? Does the future look bright or gloomy? Your feelings about the future depend more on what you think than on current circumstances. When you have a vision for tomorrow, the world becomes a better place today.*

"Every single soldier must know, before he goes into battle, how the little battle he is to fight fits into the larger picture, and how the success of his fighting will influence the battle as a whole."

—Field Marshal Bernard Montgomery

■ *It's possible to lose sight of your dream when you're working hard in the trenches. That's why it's important to always keep your eye on the big picture. Keep it before you as a daily reminder—for motivation, inspiration, and direction.*

"A blind man's world is bounded by the limits of his touch; an ignorant man's world by the limits of his knowledge; a great man's world by the limits of his vision."

—E. Paul Hovey

■ *There is really only one thing standing between you and everything you can be—and that's your dream. Never be afraid to dream too big. Enlarge yourself by growing your vision. You don't want to look back in thirty years and say, "If only I had dreamed for more. . . ."*

"Do not follow where the path may lead. Follow God, instead, where there is no path and leave a trail."

—Author Unknown

■ God desires a unique destiny for your life, not a run-of-the-mill destination. There's no way to know where He intends to lead you, but there's only one way to get there: Follow where He leads, and leave the rest to Him.

"A leader is one who sees more than others see, who sees farther than others see, and who sees before others do."

—Leroy Eims,
*Be the Leader
You Were Meant to Be*

■ *Not everyone with a dream is a leader, but every leader does have vision. To make dreams come true for themselves and their people, leaders must continually look forward. They must know where they are going, understand how to get there, and be able to lead the way.*

"You have never tested God's resources until you have attempted the impossible."

—Author Unknown

■ *Never wait for a miracle. Go after your dream. Do your part to the very best of your ability, and ask God to make up the difference. He won't act until we step out in faith.*

"As important as your past is, it is not as important as the way you see your future."

—Author Unknown

■ *The best way to seek a positive future is to look forward to it. If you're always looking over your shoulder, you won't go far before you start bumping into things. But when you believe that great things are ahead and meet each day with eager anticipation, you're creating incredible opportunities for success.*

"What would be worse than being born blind?
To have sight with no vision."

—Helen Keller

■ *God has created every person
with a purpose. But not everyone
discovers what that purpose is.
To find out, get to know
yourself—your strengths and
weaknesses. Look at your
opportunities. Examine where
God has put you. Then seek His
counsel. He will give you a vision
for your life.*

"Cherish your visions and your dreams as they are the children of your soul; the blueprints of your ultimate achievements."

—Napoleon Hill

■ *In life, we must make many trade-offs to get to the highest level. We trade being accepted by others to achieve excellence. We trade financial gain for the promise of greater potential. We trade security for the hope of increased significance. But we should never trade away our dreams. Nothing can take the place of them. And nothing holds greater hope for our future.*

"**B**ig thinking precedes great achievement."

—Wilferd A. Peterson

■ *No person has done anything great without first dreaming great dreams. Let your mind go. Think outside the lines! And don't let anyone tell you to think small. Go in a new direction. After all, you'll never succeed beyond your wildest dreams—unless you have some pretty wild dreams.*

"Inspiration without perspiration is a daydream; perspiration without inspiration is a nightmare."

—Author Unknown

■ Forty percent of the people you meet have great ideas, but they will do little more than talk about them. Another 40 percent work very hard and would be willing to give their all to a great idea, but they don't see far beyond the present moment. The remaining 20 percent possess both a dream and the will to make their dream come true. If you are a part of that remarkable 20 percent, there are no guarantees that you will be successful—but you've got a good chance, better than 80 percent of your friends have.

"Dissatisfaction and discouragement are not caused by the absence of *things* but the absence of *vision*."

—Author Unknown

■ *If life isn't looking especially wonderful today, then step back from your circumstances for a moment. Then ask yourself this question: "Why am I doing what I'm doing?" If you don't have a ready answer, then maybe you've lost sight of your vision. Do what you must to recapture your dream. It puts everything you do into perspective and keeps your thinking positive.*

"There are only two kinds of people in this world—the realists and the dreamers. The realists know where they're going. The dreamers have already been there."

—Robert Orben

■ *Where have you been lately in your dreams? Your future is likely to be only as exciting as your answer to that question. Explore your possibilities in your thoughts. Take the journey in your dreams. Then wake up and prepare to make them happen.*

"**A** #2 pencil and a dream can take you anywhere."

—J. Meyers

■ *Always keep paper and something to write with close at hand—whether you're at work, at home, or traveling. I've kept a pen and legal pad next to my bed for years because the greatest ideas I've ever received came when God awakened me in the middle of the night. The first couple of times God communicated with me that way, I didn't write them down, and in the morning, they were gone forever. But then I started putting those thoughts on paper. And because of that, I've had the privilege of seeing many of them become reality.*

"Safe living generally makes for regrets later on. We are all given talents and dreams. Sometimes the two don't match. But more often than not, we compromise both before ever finding out. Later on, as successful as we might be, we find ourselves looking back longingly to that time when we should have chased our *true* dreams and our *true* talents for all they were worth. Don't let yourself be pressured into thinking that your dreams or your talents aren't prudent. They were never meant to be prudent. They were meant to bring joy and fulfillment into your life."

—Author Unknown

■ *There is almost nothing you can't do. Look at the gifts and talents God has given you, and follow your heart. Live outrageously beyond your wildest expectations.*

"The reason we aren't living our dreams is *inside ourselves*. We only *pretend* it's people, things, and situations *outside ourselves* that are to blame."

—Author Unknown

■ *The next time you find yourself thinking that someone or something is keeping you from realizing your dream, stop yourself. If you have a dream, and you want it bad enough, you'll make it happen. Look to yourself to clear away the barriers between you and your destiny. Then determine to reach your dream no matter what it takes.*

Walt Disney never let practical realities get in the way of his imagination. "It's my job to dream the dreams," he once said, chuckling. "But paying for 'em? That's my brother Roy's job."

■ *Rarely does anyone achieve a dream alone. Walt and Roy Disney had a great partnership, each bringing to the team invaluable qualities needed by the other to succeed. So if you're having trouble keeping your eye on the dream because obstacles keep getting in the way, find someone who shares your dream and loves to eliminate obstacles, and take the journey together.*

"Here is the test to find whether your mission on earth is finished. If you're alive, it isn't."

—Richard Bach

■ *Never give up on your dream. And don't expect to one day "arrive" so that you can stop living or growing. Live each moment, day, week, year, to the fullest. Your mission in life isn't through until you're through.*

"People don't like to see others pursuing their dreams—it reminds them of how far from living their dreams *they* are. In talking you out of your dreams, they are talking themselves back into their own comfort zone. They will give you every rational lie they ever gave themselves."

—Author Unknown

■ *Don't allow yourself to be influenced by people who have given up. Love them. Help them if you can. But don't let their thinking get into your head and heart.*

"To bury our dreams is to bury ourselves, for we are really 'such stuff as dreams are made on.' God's dream for us is to reach our potential."

—Author Unknown

■ *All you do in life depends on you—on what you think you can do. The size of your dreams determines the scope of your accomplishment. Your potential has no limits. You are capable of climbing a thousand Mount Everests.*

"One can never consent to creep when one feels an impulse to soar."

—Helen Keller

■ *God gives each one of us the desire to soar. We are created in His image, which means we were not meant to creep. Fan into flame your highest ideals, your greatest God-given desires, and let them take wing. You were designed for the heights.*

"You are never given a wish without also being given the power to make it true. You may have to work for it, however."

—Richard Bach

■ *The road to your potential is open and waiting for you. It offers you the opportunity to travel to almost anywhere. But just as a trip cannot be made until you take the first step, so your dream can only come true when you start to work at it. Don't let your dream remain just potential. Start working today. Do what you can at this moment. Don't worry about what you can't yet do. Tomorrow will come soon enough.*

"Dreams become reality when we keep our commitments to them."

—Judy Wardell Halliday,
Weight Control Expert

■ *Most people think of themselves as being dedicated to achieving their dreams. But what does that really mean? What must you do to achieve your dream? What will you have to give up in order to go up? What daily disciplines will you have to develop to make your dream a reality? Are you doing them now? Commitment starts with what you're doing today. If you're not acting, you're not really committed.*

"Most men die from the neck up at age twenty-five because they stop dreaming."

—Ben Franklin

■ *Never allow yourself to get too comfortable in life. Don't plan to "arrive" by age twenty-five (or forty-five or sixty-five). The moment you think you're set for life, you start to die. Instead, keep hoping and dreaming. Seek new challenges. Develop your potential. Never outlive your dreams.*

"We grow by dreams. All big [individuals] are dreamers. They see things in the soft haze of a spring day, or in the red fire on a long winter's evening. Some of us let those great dreams die, but others nourish and protect them; nourish them through bad days until they bring them to the sunshine and light which comes always to those who sincerely hope that their dreams will come true."

—Woodrow Wilson

■ *Dreams are fragile things. My friend Bobb Biehl says they are like soap bubbles floating by rocks on a windy day. That's why you have to protect them and carry them along until they can withstand the stormy gusts of criticism, change, and cynicism. But a worthy dream, nurtured to full bloom, is an incredible thing that can change the world.*

"We all live under the same sky, but we don't all have the same horizon."

—Konrad Adenauer

■ Look at a half dozen people who are born into similar circumstances and who have the same kind of opportunities in life. You'll probably find that no two people end up the same way. The dreams you see for yourself have a great impact on what you can accomplish. Always look to the farthest horizon, and expect great things to happen.

"Some men dream of worthy accomplishments, while others stay awake and do them."

—Author Unknown

■ *A dream is an incredible thing. It motivates and sustains you. It gives you direction and helps you know your priorities. But it ultimately doesn't mean a thing if it remains only an idea. Whatever your dream is, pick yourself up and do your best to make it come true.*

YOUR AUTHENTICITY

What does it mean to be authentic? It means your words and your actions always match. It means you speak the truth in love, even when it isn't popular or pleasant. It means people can trust you because they know where you stand and what's important to you. It means you walk the road that God has created for you, without pride but also without apologies for your integrity. Above all, it means you are yourself.

"Honesty is the first chapter of the book of wisdom."

—Thomas Jefferson

■ *Judge yourself and everything you do by honesty. That is the key to being authentic—and to being successful in whatever you do.*

"Every time you are honest and conduct yourself with honesty, a success force will drive you toward greater success. Each time you lie, even with a little white lie, there are strong forces pushing you toward failure."

—Joseph Sugarman

■ *Being authentic with everyone begins with truth in all things, especially the little things. Guard yourself from making small compromises in your integrity. Small cracks are what lead to a big breakdown.*

"It is better to deserve honors and not have them than to have them and not deserve them."

—Mark Twain

■ *Fame can look very appealing, but don't make it your aim. As a goal, it's hollow and brings no satisfaction. Instead, focus on excellence, and if recognition comes, so be it.*

"If a thousand people say something foolish, it's still foolish. Truth is never dependent on consensus of opinion."

—Author Unknown

■ *It's not always easy to stand strong when the current of public opinion is flooding against you. But truth will never fail you. It is a solid rock and a safe haven in the river of ever-changing fashion.*

"The best way to promote unity is to promote truth."

—Author Unknown

■ *The only thing that the truth divides is the light from the dark, the pure from the flawed, the good from the evil. Truth is a rallying force among those who honor it.*

"Men occasionally stumble over the truth, but most of them pick themselves up and hurry off as if nothing had happened."

—Winston Churchill

■ *As you proceed in life, you will occasionally find yourself face-to-face with truth, and it will be blocking your path. Don't avoid or dismiss those moments, for it is in those times that you build character. Be authentic, and allow truth to deal with you. Once you do, you will discover that you can travel farther and climb higher than you otherwise would have been able to.*

"Follow the truth wherever it may lead."

—Thomas Jefferson

■ *Everyday life is a well-beaten roadway. But truth is like a light shining in the wilderness. Strike out for it on the narrow path, and don't let anyone convince you to give up its pursuit.*

"Prefer a loss to a dishonest gain; the one brings pain at the moment, the other for all time."

—Chilon

■ *No matter how appealing shortcuts may look, don't take them. They never pay off in the long run. The worst of all shortcuts are the ones that chip away at your character. No kind of gain—whether it be in power, relationships, possessions, or position—is worth the price of your integrity and authenticity.*

"I often wonder why scandal runs while truth must crawl."

—Author Unknown

■ *The world may not rush to hear truth, but that in no way diminishes the strength of its message. Even if others generate gossip, recount rumors, or celebrate scandal, dedicate yourself to truth.*

"A man can't be always defending the truth; there must be a time to feed on it."

—C. S. Lewis

■ *Spend time each day with the One who is the Truth. He will feed your soul, purify your heart, and strengthen your character. If you look honestly into the eyes of Jesus every day, you cannot help but be authentic with others.*

"I never give 'em hell. I just tell the truth, and they think it's hell."

—Harry S. Truman

■ *The truth doesn't hurt a person who's authentic. Everything we see is filtered through who we are. If your conscience cries out when another person speaks truth, examine yourself and look at your motives before objecting to what he or she has to say.*

"Truth is tough. It will not break."

—Oliver Wendell Holmes, Sr.

■ *Authenticity and transparency bring resiliency and stamina. Look at Jesus. He withstood gibes, taunts, humiliation, and torture. He even suffered death on a cross, yet He could not be broken. If you want to go the distance, be like Jesus.*

"Better to be occasionally cheated than perpetually suspicious."

—B. C. Forbes

■ *What we receive in life depends on the attitude we have. That's especially true when it comes to people. We can reach out to others, believing the best of them, valuing each person as important. Or we can be distrustful and skeptical, drawing away from others because we believe that they are out to hurt us. The latter may save us some pain, but it certainly will rob us of joy.*

"We thought we could trust the military,

but then came Vietnam;

We thought we could trust the politicians,

but then came Watergate;

We thought we could trust the engineers,

but then came the *Challenger* disaster;

We thought we could trust our broker,

but then came Black Monday;

We thought we could trust the preachers,

but then came PTL and Jimmy Swaggart.

So who can I trust?"

—Bill Kynes,
"A Hope That Will Not Disappoint"

■ *When we put our trust in any person, we will be disappointed. God is the only One worthy of our faith and hope.*

"Truth can be denied, but it cannot be avoided."

—Author Unknown

■ *Many people today don't believe in truth. They ask, "What is truth?" believing that each person creates his or her own. But truth doesn't depend on fashion or opinion. It stands solid as a rock, remaining forever unchanged, whether we recognize it or not.*

"The circumstances amid which you live
determine your reputation;

The truth you believe determines your character.
Reputation is what you are supposed to be;

Character is what you are. . . .
Reputation is what you have when you come to
a new community;

Character is what you have when you go
away.
Your reputation is made in a moment;

Your character is built in a lifetime. . . .
Reputation is what men say about you on your
tombstone;

Character is what the angels say about you
before the throne of God."

—William Hersey Davis

■ *Seek truth as the foundation of*
all you believe and everything
you do. Take care of your
character, and let your reputation
take care of itself.

"You don't really know a person until you have observed his behavior with a child, a flat tire, when the boss is away, and when he thinks no one will ever know."

—Author Unknown

■ *When you are truly authentic, then you are the same person no matter who you're with—your friends, boss, clients, parents, children, pastor. . . . You may relate to people where they are, but your values and priorities remain the same, even when you are all alone.*

"Character is like a tree and reputation like its shadow. The shadow is what we think of it; the tree is the real thing."

—Abraham Lincoln

■ *Never confuse what others think of you with who you really are. Be humble and authentic in everything you do, and you will never be left chasing shadows.*

"People show what they are by what they do with what they have."

—Author Unknown

■ *We can look at what God's given us*
and harp on what we're lacking;
Or celebrate the gifts we have,
embrace them, and get cracking.

"You can't get much done in life if you only work on the days when you feel good."

—Jerry West

■ *Good character is never based on feelings. It means doing your best when you feel the worst, loving others when they break your heart, and going the extra mile even when you were barely able to finish the first.*

"For when the One Great Scorer comes
to write against your name,
He marks—not that you won or lost—
but how you played the game."

—Grantland Rice

■ *People today are obsessed with winning. Some will do anything to come in first, even if it means compromising their integrity and authenticity. But God is more concerned with our good character than the number of goals we score. Play to come in first, but don't lose yourself in order to win the game.*

"No man can tell whether he is rich or poor by turning to his ledger. It is the heart that makes a man rich. He is rich according to what he is, not according to what he has."

—Henry Ward Beecher

If you want to know the true wealth of a person, don't look at what she has. Look at what she gives away. That is a better indication of the person's heart for God and other people.

"How a man plays the game shows something of his character; how he loses shows all of it."

—Camden County (Georgia) *Tribune*

■ *Everyone experiences fumbles, flops, and failures in life. They are inevitable. What isn't inevitable is that they stop you. When you fall, learn from it and get back up again.*

"No man can for any considerable time wear one face to himself and another to the multitude without finally getting bewildered as to which is the true one."

—Nathaniel Hawthorne

■ *Don't try to be someone else or pretend to be someone you're not. Just do your best to be the person God created you to be. Nothing more, nothing less.*

"Everybody ought to do at least two things each day that he hates to do, just for the practice."

—William James

■ *No matter how successful you become in life, keep your feet firmly on the ground. How do you do that? Continue doing the things you don't like but ought to do. It will help you maintain your perspective, develop character, and keep growing.*

YOUR FRIENDSHIPS

What things are worth living and dying for? If asked, could you narrow your list down to three or four? If friendships aren't already on your short list, I want to encourage you to add them.

The relationships you build make a huge difference in your life, and they're worth the hard work it takes to keep them. Start with your family: your spouse and your children. Then extend yourself to others. Build those important relationships, and make giving yourself a top priority. If you want to enjoy the journey and go a long distance, take somebody with you.

"I can do what you can't do, and you can do what I can't do. *Together* we can do great things."

—Mother Teresa

■ *There's almost no limit to what people can do together. As you look for people to join you in accomplishing your dreams, find people who complement your strengths and offset your weaknesses. In that way, both you and they will be able to go farther than you ever could alone.*

"One of the realities of life is that if you can't trust a person at all points, you can't truly trust him or her at any point."

—Cheryl Biehl

■ *When seeking out a friend, look first for integrity. It is the glue that holds relationships together. With it, a friendship can weather just about any storm. Without it, even in the mildest conditions it can't last.*

"Trust most those who stand to lose as much as you when things go wrong."

—Author Unknown

Just about anyone can stand on the sidelines and give advice. But a partner who is in the game with you has a vested interest in whether you fail or succeed. Listen to him with extra care.

"There is no limit to what can be done if it doesn't matter who gets the credit."

—Author Unknown

■ *When you reach a milestone or accomplish something significant, do you try to grab all the credit, or do you give it away to others? If your desire is to always be in the spotlight, you will find fewer and fewer people willing to join you in achieving your dreams. But when you give the credit away, not only do you get more accomplished, but everything you do helps to build your momentum. And you won't have to look far for people to partner with, because others will seek you out. Everyone loves to work with a person who shares the spotlight.*

"In prosperity our friends know us. In adversity we know our friends."

—Author Unknown

■ *Think about the last time you were in trouble. Who was there for you? Who loved you when you were at your most unlovable? Who wanted to be with you when you had nothing to give? Those people are your friends. Always cherish and nurture your relationships with them.*

"Friendship multiplies joys and divides grief."

—Author Unknown

> ■ *Friendship is a great gift.*
> *Friends help us savor and*
> *celebrate our victories. When we*
> *fall, they help us up. And in times*
> *of trouble, they encourage us and*
> *help us carry the load. As King*
> *Solomon said: Two are truly*
> *better than one.*

"No one can help everybody, but everyone can help someone."

—Author Unknown

■ *If you want to change the world, you can only do it one person at a time. Start wherever you are, and help the people around you. Help your family, your neighbor, your friend. The opportunities are there; you only need to look for them.*

"The only people you should try to get even with are those who have helped you."

—Author Unknown

■ *Forgive and forget about the people who've hurt you. Instead, try to return the love, grace, and kindness you've been shown. You can never truly "get even," because what you've received is a gift. But you can pass it on to others.*

"My friends didn't believe that I could become a successful speaker. So I did something about it. I went out and found me some new friends!"

—Joe Larson, Professional Speaker

■ *Sometimes we need to do something radical to break through to the next level in life. If the people around you don't believe in you, if they don't encourage you, then you need to find some people who do. Love everybody, but only make close friends of the people who want to see you reach your potential.*

"Friendship is built upon the commitment to be a friend, not upon the desire to have a friend."

—Author Unknown

■ *Giving is the highest level of living. It is also the basis of friendship. When both people approach the relationship with an attitude of giving, there's almost no limit to where that friendship can take them.*

G eneral William Westmoreland was once reviewing a platoon of paratroopers in Vietnam. As he went down the line, he asked each of them a question: "How do you like jumping, son?" "Love it, sir!" was the first answer. "How do you like jumping?" he asked the next. "The greatest experience in my life, sir!" exclaimed the paratrooper. "How do you like jumping?" he asked the third. "I hate it, sir," he replied. "Then why do you do it?" asked Westmoreland. "Because I want to be around the guys who love to jump."

■ *Surround yourself with people who energize and inspire you, and you can accomplish anything.*

"Your best friend is he who brings out the best that is within you."

—Henry Ford

■ *What is a "best friend"? Is it the person who makes you laugh the most? Is it the one who gives you the best advice? Or is it the one who makes you feel good? No, it's the person who helps you reach your potential. Sometimes that person does make you laugh and feel good. But other times he or she looks you in the eye and tells you what you don't want to hear. A best friend is willing to do whatever it takes to help you become the person God created you to be.*

I f you isolate yourself from other people, you are two to three times more likely to die an early death, even if you take good care of yourself by exercising or refraining from smoking.

- If you isolate yourself from others, you are more likely to contract terminal cancer.
- If you are divorced, separated, or widowed, you have a five to ten times greater chance of being hospitalized for a mental disorder than if you are married.
- If you are a pregnant woman without good personal relationships, your chances of having some kind of complication are three times as great as those with strong relationships, even given the same amount of stress.

—California Department
of Mental Health

■ *The medical profession is only just beginning to document what people have known instinctively for years: Good relationships affect every area of people's lives in a positive way.*

"Friendship consists of a willing ear, an understanding heart, and a helping hand."

—Frank Tyger

■ *What kind of attitude do you bring to the relationships in your life? Are you a giver or a taker? Are you a listener, or are you doing most of the talking? Do you seek to understand or to be understood? The greatest gift you can give to another is yourself.*

"A mirror reflects a man's face, but what he is really like is shown by the kind of friends he chooses."

—King Solomon

■ *Think about the people with whom you spend most of your time. What are the best four or five words you would use to describe them? Did you realize that those same words could also be used to describe you? Even if they are not totally accurate today, they will be in time. What Charles "Tremendous" Jones says is true. Who you will be in the future is strongly affected by the people you associate with.*

"Friends are made by many acts—they can be lost by one."

—Author Unknown

■ *Have you lost a friend recently because of something you did or said that hurt the person? If you have, take time to repair the broken relationship. Ask for forgiveness and try, as far as it's in your power, to make things right. True friends are worth fighting to keep.*

"The glory of friendship is not in the outstretched hand, nor the kindly smile, nor the joy of companionship; it is in the spiritual inspiration that comes to one when he discovers that someone else believes in him and is willing to trust him."

—Ralph Waldo Emerson

■ *Give your confidence and trust to someone close to you. Tell that person today how much you believe in her or him. Both of you will be better for it.*

"After you've made the winning basket, you've got 15,000 people cheering for you, TV stations coming at you, and everybody giving you high-fives. You don't need me then. When you need a real friend is when you feel that nobody likes you."

—K. C. Jones,
Former Boston Celtics Coach
(Quoted by former Celtics Player
Kevin McHale)

■ *Friends know you well and recognize your needs—sometimes even before you know them yourself.*

"People who have warm friends are healthier and happier than those who have none. A single real friend is a treasure worth more than gold or precious stones. Money can buy many things, good and evil. All the wealth of the world could not buy you a friend or pay you for the loss of one."

—C. D. Prentice

■ *Spend your time with others even more wisely than you spend your money, and you will always be rich.*

"A true friend is one who hears and understands when you share your deepest feelings. He supports you when you are struggling; he corrects you, gently and with love, when you err; and he forgives you when you fail. A true friend prods you to personal growth, stretches you to your full potential. And most amazing of all, he celebrates your successes as if they were his own."

—Richard Exley

■ *Many people are willing to cry with friends when they're feeling sad. But fewer people want to laugh with them when they experience success. True friendship knows no jealousy. A friend will offer you a shoulder to lean on after a defeat, and he'll put you on his shoulders to celebrate after a victory.*

D wight Morrow, the father of Anne Morrow Lindbergh, once held a dinner party to which Calvin Coolidge had been invited. After Coolidge left, Morrow told the remaining guests that Coolidge would make a good president. The others disagreed. They felt Coolidge was too quiet, that he lacked color and personality. No one would like him, they said.

Anne, then age six, spoke up. "I like him," she said. Then she displayed a finger with a small bandage around it. "He was the only one at the party who asked about my sore finger."

"And that's why he would make a good president," said Morrow.

■ *Give each person you meet the care and attention you would a friend, and everyone you meet will be a friend.*

"Spread love everywhere you go: first of all in your own house. Give love to your children, to your wife or husband, to a next door neighbor. . . . Let no one ever come to you without leaving better and happier. Be the living expression of God's kindness; kindness in your face, kindness in your eyes, kindness in your smile, kindness in your warm greeting."

—Mother Teresa

■ *Never lose sight of the fact that your most important relationships are at home. Spend time nurturing and developing them every day. And then let the love that starts there overflow into the rest of your life.*

"The measure of a man is not the number of people who serve him, but the number of people he serves."

—Author Unknown

■ *When was the last time you took an inventory of what you've given to others instead of what you've received? Not that we are to keep score, but it's a good reminder that we should be giving more than getting. When all is said and done, any honor we receive will come from how we have served, not how we were served.*

YOUR POSSIBILITIES

You stand at a unique crossroads. You are the only person in the history of humanity with your particular background, experience, and talents. The world has waited until this moment for your arrival. Your possibilities are almost limitless. What do you plan to do with this opportunity? You're only going to get one chance—the one you have right now. Vow to make the most of it. Strive to reach your potential. Expand your possibilities. Make every moment count.

"More men fail through lack of purpose than lack of talent."

—Billy Sunday

■ *Talent is highly overrated. On any given day, you'll probably meet well over a dozen people whose talents exceed your own. Of greater worth is a sense of purpose. That's what gives you power. The paychecks of innumerable talented people are signed by people of purpose.*

"Hell begins on that day when God grants us a clear vision of all that we might have achieved, of all the gifts we wasted, of all that we might have done that we did not do."

—Gian Carlo Menotti, Composer
(Quoted by Og Mandino in
The Return of the Ragpicker)

■ *Don't wait to begin growing and reaching your potential. Take the next logical step in the development process. Start today with whatever resources you have available. Become the person you are destined to be.*

"You cannot strengthen the weak by weakening the strong.

You cannot help small men by tearing down big men.

You cannot help the poor by destroying the rich.

You cannot lift the wage earner by pulling down the wage payer.

You cannot keep out of trouble by spending more than your income.

You cannot further the brotherhood of man by inciting class hatreds.

You cannot establish security on borrowed money.

You cannot build character and courage by taking away a man's incentive and independence.

You cannot help men permanently by doing for them what they could and should do themselves."

—Abraham Lincoln

■ *The key to achieving your destiny lies in building up others. It is only as we pour ourselves into other people that we succeed.*

"The greatest obstacle to discovery is not ignorance. It is the illusion of knowledge."

—Author Unknown

■ *When will you come to the end of your possibilities? Here's the answer: the moment you believe you've learned everything you need to know. It isn't what we don't know that stops us from succeeding. It's what we think we do know. Become a lifelong learner, and you'll never run out of possibilities.*

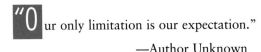

"Our only limitation is our expectation."

—Author Unknown

■ *What do you believe you are capable of? How far do you think you can go? It may surprise you to know that your attitude does more to determine your future than anything else in life: talent, resources, connections, or opportunities. If you believe you can, you can!*

"More and more people today have the means to live but no meaning to live for."

—Victor Frankl

■ *Don't let the trappings of life distract you from the meaning of life. Cars, houses, bank accounts, technology—none of these mean a thing. What's important is that you love God and love your neighbor. Everything else is secondary.*

"To make your life small when it could be great is sin and heresy."

—Elton Trueblood

■ *Think in terms of your highest potential. We are told in Scripture to seek the greater gifts, not the lesser ones. Desire excellence. Grow. Aim for the top in everything you do. Don't miss the opportunity to become the best person you can be.*

"The greatest use of life is to use it so that it outlives you. Live and give of yourself to a cause greater than yourself."

—Author Unknown

■ So often we think about life in terms of what's happening today, this week, or next month. We need to try to look at things as God does, with an eye for eternity. Is what you're doing now making a lasting impact? Will it matter in another year, another decade, another century? Begin dedicating yourself to things that will still be important long after you're gone.

"Measure your possibilities not according to what you see in yourself, but according to what you see in God for you."

—Author Unknown

■ *If you want to know who you are and what you may become, turn to God. You see yourself as you truly are only when you see yourself through God's eyes.*

"All things are possible to him who believes; they are less difficult to him who hopes; they are easy to him who loves; and they are simple to anyone who does all three."

—Brother Lawrence

■ *The first step in accomplishing the impossible is to refuse to believe it. From that point, everything else comes more easily.*

"The real contest is always between what you've done and what you're capable of doing. You measure yourself against yourself and nobody else."

—Geoffrey Gaberino,
Olympic Gold Medalist, Swimming

■ *Don't compare yourself to others. You will look at your weaknesses next to their areas of giftedness and feel demoralized, or you will put your best up against their worst and become smug. Either way you lose. Instead, think in terms of where you are compared to your potential—and then keep striving to be your best.*

"Always ask, 'Is there a better way?'"

—Author Unknown

■ *Nothing great has ever been accomplished by someone who wanted to do things the way they've always been done. Don't wait for something to break before you make it better. Strive for excellence in everything you do.*

"If we don't change, we don't grow. If we don't grow, we are not really living. Growth demands a temporary surrender of security. It may mean a giving up of familiar but limiting patterns, safe but unrewarding work, values no longer believed in, relationships that have lost their meaning. As Dostoevsky put it, 'Taking a new step, uttering a new word, is what people fear most.' The real fear should be the opposite course."

—Gail Sheehy

■ *If you want to become a person of destiny, one of the best things you can do for yourself is learn to fail. Most people fear failure so much that they refuse to take risks and grow. Don't let the quicksand of fear bog you down. When you're willing to risk failure, you're finally free to reach for your goals.*

"The thing is to understand myself, to see what God really wishes me to do . . . to find the idea for which I can live and die."

—Søren Kierkegaard

■ *There are at most a handful of things worth dying for. Find out what yours are, and you will really be able to live.*

"It is nothing to die. It's an awful thing never to have lived."

—Jean Valjean, in
Victor Hugo's *Les Miserables*

■ *Live each day as if it were your last. Seize it and celebrate it. Squeeze it as if you were wringing the last drop of moisture out of a piece of cloth in the middle of the desert.*

"No individual has any right to come into the world and go out of it without leaving behind him distinct and legitimate reasons for having passed through it."

—George Washington Carver

What are you leaving behind in this world? Never mind what others have or haven't done before you. Create your own legacy. And then help your fellow man with his.

наследство

"Unhappiness is in not knowing what we want and killing ourselves to get it."

—Don Herold

■ *Most people work very hard at things they care very little about. Don't just get on the treadmill of life with everyone else. Instead, take time to discover your destiny. If you're going to work your whole life to become someone, you might as well make it the someone you want to be.*

"Some men have thousands of reasons why they cannot do what they want to, when all they need is one reason why they can."

—Willis R. Whitney

■ *Give yourself a reason to follow and fulfill your dream. All it takes is one.*

"Our souls are not hungry for fame, comfort, wealth, or power. Those rewards create almost as many problems as they solve. Our souls are hungry for meaning, for the sense that we have figured out how to live so that our lives matter, so that the world will at least be a little bit different for our having passed through it."

—Harold Kushner

■ *It takes most people some time to discover what God created them for. But as soon as you've made that discovery, change your focus from success to significance. Don't try to impress; instead, impact. Seek influence; not affluence. Don't try to make just money; make a difference.*

"All of life is lived on levels and arrived at in stages."

—Ed Cole

■ *Life is an uphill journey. No matter where you start in life or where you're going, it takes effort to make it to the next level. If you're not willing to push yourself, then get used to the scenery where you are. You may be there a long time.*

"Learn as if you were to live forever.
Live as if you were to die tomorrow."

—Author Unknown

■ *One of the secrets of living a full life is to plan for tomorrow but live for today. One of the best ways to do that is to practice disciplines and pursue opportunities every day. Daily disciplines are the key to growth and personal development. The ability to seize opportunities makes it possible for you to make the most of everything God has given you. Disciplines prepare you to go to the next level. Opportunities allow you to make the trip.*

"Progress in life is not measured by security but by growth; and growth means taking occasional risks. You'll never get anywhere interesting by always doing the safe thing."

—Author Unknown

■ *Any totally safe road you find will lead only to stagnation. Life is a series of choices and chances. It requires faith and action. You can't stay in the harbor and discover new worlds at the same time.*

"The secret of success is consistency of purpose."

—Benjamin Disraeli

■ *Once you discover your purpose in life, focus your attention there. Change from generalist to specialist. You cannot be a person of destiny and a jack-of-all-trades at the same time.*

YOUR CHOICES

Nothing will have a greater impact on your future than the choices you make today—not the state of society, the condition of the government, the health of the economy, or anything else. Those things are outside of your control. What is under your control is what you choose to do—or not to do. Each time you make a choice, you move a little farther in a particular direction, for good or for ill. Choose wisely, and the bridge you build will take you to the future you desire.

"Keep on going and the chances are you will stumble on something, perhaps when you are least expecting it. I have never heard of anyone stumbling on something sitting down."

—Charles F. Kettering

■ *One of the most important choices you'll ever make is how you will approach life on a day-to-day basis. You can sit back and wait for things to happen, or you can go out and make them happen. The choice is yours.*

"When, against one's will, one is high-pressured into making a hurried decision, the best answer is always 'No,' because 'No' is more easily changed to 'Yes' than 'Yes' is changed to 'No.'"

—Charles E. Nielsen

■ *Any time a choice will help you realize your vision, it's easy to give the right answer. But if someone is pushing you in a direction you're not sure of, graciously decline. A single opportunity missed hurts your momentum less than one poor opportunity pursued.*

"Cowardice asks the question: Is it safe?
Consensus asks the question: Is it popular?
Conscience asks: Is it right?"

—Martin Luther King, Jr.

■ *The questions people ask when they're preparing to make a decision can tell us a lot about their character. Are they looking for security or growth? Is self-preservation their greatest desire, or are they looking out for the organization? Is money their main concern, or are they thinking first about people? Listen carefully and you'll understand a lot.*

"Bill, you're going to find that 95 percent of all the decisions you'll ever make in your career could be made as well by any reasonably intelligent high school sophomore. But they'll pay you for the other 5 percent."

—Spoken by Marion Folsom,
Eastman Kodak Executive,
to Williard C. Butcher,
Chairman, Chase Manhattan
Corporation

Don't waste your time agonizing over unimportant things; save your energy for the crucial ones. Try to make sure every problem is solved at the lowest possible level in your organization. As you rise to the top, your decisions should be fewer and bigger.

"If you don't make up your mind, then your unmade mind will unmake you."

—E. Stanley Jones

■ *Always remember that when you refuse to make a decision, that in itself is a decision. The greatest power you have is the power to choose. You certainly don't have to do anything in life, but you are accountable for whatever you don't do.*

"It's not hard to make decisions when you know what your values are."

—Roy Disney

■ *Never make decisions outside of the context of your values. Every choice you make must be consistent with your deepest beliefs, or you will erode your integrity and your freedom to make choices in the future.*

"Wherever you see a successful business, someone once made a courageous decision."

—Peter Drucker

■ *People who rely on luck and believe it is the key to success are some of the unluckiest people you'll ever meet. Success comes as the result of hard work and tough choices. Ask any successful businessperson what his or her turning point was, and the person will probably tell you about making a courageous decision sometime in the past.*

"My obligation is to do the right thing. The rest is in God's hands."

—Martin Luther King, Jr.

■ *As you face a decision, always determine what the right thing is to do. If you do that first, then a choice is often very easy to make.*

"Those who do not create the future they want must endure the future they get."

—Author Unknown

■ *Life is a journey, a process. Every day you must deliberately make the effort to take a few steps. Learn, grow, become better than you are today. The secret of your future is hidden in your daily routine.*

"When you come to a fork in the road, take it."

—Yogi Berra

■ *Don't wait for everything to be perfect before you're willing to make decisions. If you do, you'll always be waiting, and you'll never move forward in the journey of life. For every major fork in the road, there comes a time when you have to make a choice based on the information you have. Make the best choice you can and then move on.*

"Once a decision is reached, stop worrying and start working."

—William James

■ *You can't accomplish anything of significance if you're second guessing your every move.*

"Three choices a person has concerning things that bother him/her:

1. Deal with it.
2. Get over it.
3. Learn to live with it."

—Jack Murray

■ *Life is really much simpler that we often make it out to be. Whenever you have a problem, rather than agonizing over it, think about what Jack Murray says. You can solve it, decide not to let it bother you, or adapt to it. Sooner or later you have to do one of those things, so you might as well choose.*

*H*ave you ever wondered how to prioritize the choices you make in life? Take a look at the following list of questions. They represent the five greatest choices you will ever make in your life, other than how you will respond to Jesus Christ:

> How much education will you obtain?
> Who will you marry?
> If you marry, will you have children and if so, how many?
> What will be your vocation in life?
> Where will you live?

"When you cannot make up your mind which of two evenly balanced courses of action you should take—choose the bolder."

—General W. J. Slim

■ *At the end of life, there are no rewards for being dull or ordinary. Travel the road less taken to your destiny. It truly does make a difference.*

"We all have the power of choice, but once used, our choice has power over us. Weigh the consequences of your choices."

—Author Unknown

■ *When we are born, nearly everything in our lives is outside of our control. But as we get older, we become increasingly responsible for ourselves. Who you and I currently are is the result of all the choices we've made up until now. And the choices you're making today, at this very moment, are forming the person you will be tomorrow.*

"You've got to think about the 'big things' while you're doing small things, so that all the small things go in the right direction."

—Alvin Toffler

■ *Never lose sight of the big picture when making choices. If you can't see the forest for the trees, you're almost certain to get lost.*

"God never puts anyone in a place too small to grow."

—Author Unknown

■ *It's human nature to think that the person you admire sitting next to you has it better than you do. But God doesn't see it that way. Everyone is different. To some people He gives five talents, to some two, and to others one. How many you received doesn't matter. The question is, "What are you going to do with what you've got?"*

"No matter how little or how much a job pays us in money, if we do not also derive from that work the satisfaction of doing something important, we have made a bad bargain."

—Author Unknown

■ *Don't settle for a life that feeds your body but starves your soul. Do something that matters. If you're not currently doing that, then create a plan to make changes in your life and work as hard as you can to make them happen.*

"Choice, not chance, determines destiny."

—*The Bible Friend*

■ *Luck is a myth, and there is no such thing as coincidence. Our choices determine 80 percent of what we do in life and 100 percent of our attitude toward it.*

A prominent salesman summed up his success in three simple words—"and then some." "I discovered at an early age," he said, "that most of the differences between average and top people could be explained in three words. The top people did what was expected of them—and then some. They were thoughtful of others; they were considerate and kind—and then some. They met their obligations and responsibilities fairly and squarely—and then some. They were good friends to their friends, and could be counted on in an emergency—and then some."

—Author Unknown

■ *If you put other people first, and make excellence the standard in everything you do, you'll really be living—and then some.*

"If we did all the things we are capable of doing, we would literally astonish ourselves."

—Thomas Edison

■ *Most people have no idea how far below their potential they're living. God has created us with almost limitless possibilities. If you look at your life and you aren't just a little surprised by how far you've come, then you probably aren't growing at the rate you should, and it's time to try the impossible. As Eleanor Roosevelt said, "Do the thing you think you cannot do."*

YOUR CONTRIBUTION

If your epitaph were being written today, how would it read? What would it say about you and what you are leaving behind? Would it describe how you touched the world in a positive way, or would it be blank? You may not think of it often, but your epitaph really is being written today—and you're writing it. It is the sum of all you say and do each day. So give all you can to whomever you can. Leave the world better than you found it.

"No man can live happily who regards himself alone, who turns everything to his own advantage. You must live for others if you wish to live for yourself."

—Seneca

■ Only as we serve others do we make a lasting contribution to our world. As Robert South said, "If there be any truer measure of a man than by what he does, it must be what he gives."

"It is not the critic who counts; not the man who points out how the strong man stumbled, or where the doer of deeds could have done better. The credit belongs to the man who is actually in the arena, whose face is marred by dust and sweat and blood: who strives valiantly; who errs and comes short again and again; who knows the great enthusiasms, the great devotions and spends himself in a worthy cause; who at the best knows in the end the triumph of high achievement; and who at the worst if he fails, at least fails while doing greatly; so that his place shall never be with those cold and timid souls who know neither victory or defeat."

—Theodore Roosevelt

■ *Don't stand on the sidelines of life criticizing the performance of others. Get into the game.*

"How wonderful it is that nobody need wait a single minute before starting to improve the world."

—Anne Frank

■ *Occasionally I hear people say that they intend to begin helping others someday in the future. They'll work with the homeless, give to their church, support a missionary, feed a starving child—tomorrow, when they have the money, time, etc. But often tomorrow becomes next week, next week becomes next year, and next year becomes "when the children grow up" or "when I retire." No matter what you hope to do, begin in some way today. Who knows what tomorrow holds?*

"Don't judge each day by the harvest you reap but by the seeds you plant."

—Robert Louis Stevenson

■ *Most people judge themselves and others by the size of their harvest. How much did she make last year? How big a contract did he sign? How much has his organization grown? What kind of car did they buy? It takes great effort to change our mind-set and approach to life from getting to giving. The next time you're tempted to figure out how much you can get, ask yourself how much you are able to give.*

"Pleasure in the job puts perfection in the work."

—Aristotle

■ *When you enjoy your work and make it a positive experience, it inspires you to excellence. Remember that, not only for yourself, but for the people you lead.*

"My grandfather once told me that there are two kinds of people: those who do the work and those who take the credit. He told me to try to be in the first group; there was much less competition there."

—Indira Gandhi

■ *Not only is there less competition, but there are greater rewards.*

"Do not tell me how hard you work. Tell me how much you get done."

—James J. Ling

■ *To succeed certainly requires work, but hard work alone does not guarantee success. Digging ditches is about the hardest work a person can find, but doing that every day will only get you holes and a sore back. You have to measure results. As my friend Bill Purvis says, "Don't tell me about your aches and pains; just show me the baby."*

"Forget yourself into greatness. Empty yourself into adventure. Lose yourself into immortality."

—William Arthur Ward,
Texas Wesleyan College

■ *Life can be a great adventure,
but only if you make it one.*

"No man becomes rich unless he enriches others."

—Andrew Carnegie

Andrew Carnegie was one of the richest men in the world in his day, and he made it his goal to invest his money in others. In all, he gave away more than $350 million. But don't worry—you don't have to be a Carnegie or a Rockefeller to enrich others. Give what you can of what you have.

"When you give your best to the world, the world returns the favor."

—H. Jackson Brown, Jr.

■ *The way you see the world is the way the world sees you. If you think positively, you live in a positive world. If you give your best, others do the same for you. It's really true that what you see is what you get.*

"We have too many people who live without working, and altogether too many who work without living."

—Charles R. Brown

■ *Work and play are two of the most wonderful activities life has to offer. But either one would lose something without the other. Work hard and fulfill your destiny, but don't forget to have fun along the way. There are a lot of things that you should take seriously—but you are not one of them.*

"Let each person sweep in front of his own door, and then the whole world will be clean."

—Johann Wolfgang von Goethe

■ *Every problem you want to solve, condition you want to improve, and wrong you want to right begins with you. If you want to change the world, first change yourself.*

"A man will rust out faster than he'll wear out."

—Harland ("Colonel") Sanders

■ *Never plan to retire, no matter what age you reach. The day you decide to stop growing and contributing to your world, you begin to rust. And before long, you've lost your mettle.*

"Let us realize that the privilege to work is a gift, that power to work is a blessing, that love of work is success."

—David O. McKay

■ *Many times we don't realize the importance of our ability to work and contribute until we lose it.*

"After the cheers have died and the stadium is empty, after the headlines have been written and after you are back in the quiet of your own room and the Super Bowl ring has been placed on the dresser and all the pomp and fanfare has faded, the enduring thing that is left is the dedication to doing with our lives the very best we can to make the world a better place in which to live."

—Vince Lombardi,
Former Coach of the Green Bay Packers

■ *Pour yourself into the lives of others, whether you coach football, build appliances, wait tables, or lead people. The difference you make in people's lives is the only one that ultimately matters.*

"It is not what a man does that determines whether his work is sacred or secular, it is why he does it."

—A. W. Tozer

■ *The kind of work we do is not as important as the attitude we bring to it. We should approach every endeavor with an attitude of excellence, doing everything as if it were for the Lord Himself. That's what the apostle Paul counseled nearly two thousand years ago, and it's still good advice.*

"Most of the significant contributions that have been made to society have been made by people who were tired."

—Winston Churchill

■ *If you try to get things done only when you feel good, you simply won't ever get much done.*

"Most of the footprints on the sands of time were made by work shoes."

—Author Unknown

■ How many people known for their contribution to leisure activities are still remembered one hundred years after their death? If you want to make an impact, give yourself to work that will last by improving the lives of others.

Andrew Carnegie said that there were two types of people who never achieve very much in their lifetime. One is the person who won't do what he or she is told to do, and the other is the person who does no more than he or she is told to do.

■ *If you want to go far fast, do more than is expected of you.*

"I believe in the dignity of labor; whether with head or hand; that the world owes no man a living but that it owes every man an opportunity to make a living."

—John D. Rockefeller, Jr.

What opportunities are available to you right now? Take a look around. No matter where you are or what your circumstances may be, you have great possibilities. You just need to see them and seize them.

"One of the worst mistakes you can make is to think you are working for someone else."

—Author Unknown

■ *Every person is an entrepreneur. If you aren't satisfied with the work you're doing, then send yourself to get more training so that you can do something else. If you don't like your work environment, change it, either by making adjustments where you are or moving to a new place. You hold the keys to your destiny. If you're not happy, take it up with your boss—you.*

"Seven signs of a 'work spirit':

- a sense of enormous energy
- a positive, open state of mind
- a sense of purpose and vision
- a full sense of self
- awareness of oneself as a creator and nurturer
- a sense of living in the moment
- a sense of higher order and oneness."

—Sherrie Connelly,
Organizational Consultant

■ *Work to develop a positive working spirit.*

"The heights by great men reached and kept
Were not attained by sudden flight,
But they, while their companions slept,
Were toiling upward in the night."

—Henry Wadsworth Longfellow

■ *It's been said that to be successful, all you have to do is work half-days—you can work the first twelve hours or the second twelve. There are various factors that contribute to a person's success, but hard work is almost always one of them.*

"A successful man continues to look for work after he has found a job."

—Author Unknown

■ *Always keep your eyes open to opportunities and possibilities. You don't know what will be required of you tomorrow.*

"Most people would rather get home than get ahead."

—Author Unknown

■ *You can't watch the clock and make a meaningful contribution at the same time. If you'd rather be anyplace other than your job, it's time to start looking for another place to do your job.*

"I never did a day's work in my life. It was all fun."

—Thomas A. Edison

■ *Choose what you do in life according to your passion and purpose. In the end you don't want to work for a living, you want to live for the work you're doing.*

"Nothing is work unless you'd rather be doing something else."

—George Halas

■ *The person who looks upon his work as a game always enjoys it. And he almost always plays to win.*

"Hard work without talent is a shame, but talent without hard work is a tragedy."

—Robert Half

■ *Some of the saddest words in the English language are "What might have been." Don't let a day go by without developing your potential.*

"It is wonderful how much can be done if we are always doing."

—Thomas Jefferson

■ *Inspiration and motivation are nice to have, but there is no substitute for just getting started.*

One team of researchers followed a group of 1,500 people over a period of 20 years. At the outset of the study, the participants were divided into two groups: Group A, 83 percent of the sample, was composed of people embarking on a career path they had chosen solely for the prospect of making money now in order to do what they wanted later in life.

Group B, the other 17 percent of the sample, consisted of people who had chosen their career paths so that they could do what they wanted now and worry about the money later.

The data showed some startling revelations:

- At the end of the 20 year period, 101 of the 1,500 had become millionaires.
- Of the millionaires, all but one—100 out of 101—were from Group B, the group that had chosen to pursue what they loved.

The key ingredient in most successful projects is loving what you do. Having a goal or a plan is not enough. Academic preparation is not enough. Prior experience is not enough. Enjoyment of your life's work is the key.

—Robert Kriegel and Louis Patler,
If It Ain't Broke . . . Break It

■ *Choose a job you love, and you'll be rich in body and soul.*

"I long to accomplish a great and noble task; but it is my chief duty and joy to accomplish humble tasks as though they were great and noble. The world is moved along, not only by the mighty shoves of its heroes, but also by the aggregate of the tiny pushes of each honest worker."

—Helen Keller

■ *It's not the size of her work that makes a person great, it's the nobility of her character.*

"If people knew how hard I work to get my mastery, it wouldn't seem so wonderful at all."

—Michelangelo

■ *Most of the achievements we see every day that appear to come from genius, wealth, or luck are really the results of hard work.*

"When you are making a success of something, it's not work. It's a way of life. You enjoy yourself because you are making your contribution to the world."

—Andy Granatelli

■ *God created you with a purpose in mind. Make that purpose part of you. Then make yourself part of that purpose.*

One summer evening when Thomas Edison returned from work, his wife said, "You've worked too long without a rest. You must take a vacation." "But where will I go?" he asked. "Decide where you'd rather be than anywhere else on earth and go there," was the answer. "Very well," promised Mr. Edison, "I will go tomorrow." The next morning Edison returned to his laboratory.

■ *If someone told you the same thing, where would you go?*

"First find something you like to do so much you'd gladly do it for nothing; then learn to do it so well people are happy to pay you for it."

—Walt Disney

■ *When what you do has meaning and gives you joy, it has meaning to others and gives them joy.*

"If a man is to be called a street sweeper, he should sweep streets even as Michelangelo painted, or Beethoven composed music, or Shakespeare wrote poetry. He should sweep streets so well that all the hosts of heaven and earth will pause to say, 'Here lived a great street sweeper who did his job well.'"

—Martin Luther King, Jr.

■ *Make the angels rejoice. Bring excellence to everything you do.*

YOUR FUTURE

Your future is bright. It may not look like the one your parents or your grandparents faced, but that's a good thing. You and others in your generation are blazing new trails and finding new ways to make a difference. That is how it should be. If you were happy with everything as it is, there would be no positive future. Like everyone, you will make mistakes, but a better future is built on the successes and failures of today. That gives you hope. And where there is hope for the future, there is power for the present.

"No matter what a person's past may have been, his future is spotless."

—Author Unknown

■ *Your future is a blank canvas, waiting only for you to get started on it. The picture you paint is limited only by the size of your vision, the colors you've put on your palette, and your willingness to keep working until it's done.*

"We should not let our fears hold us back from pursuing our hopes."

—John F. Kennedy

■ *Everyone experiences fear. But it hurts you only if you let it control your thinking and your actions. As you discover your dream, and prepare to take action, feel your fear but do it anyway.*

"The service we render to others is really the rent we pay for our room on this earth. It is obvious that man is himself a traveler; that the purpose of this world is not 'to have and to hold' but 'to give and serve.' There can be no other meaning."

—Sir Wilfred T. Grenfell

■ *We can never truly pay back what we receive during our time on this earth. Even life itself is a gift. But we certainly should do all we can while we're here.*

"It's not the work of life but the worry of life that robs us of strength and breaks down our faith."

—Author Unknown

■ *Work doesn't make a person tired, worry does. It saps your energy and attacks your dreams. It tries to make you believe you can't succeed when success is almost within your grasp. Win over worry, and you'll find that victory is at hand.*

"The future is that time when you'll wish you'd done what you aren't doing now."

—Author Unknown

■ *What must you do today to make your dreams become a reality in the future? Break it down. What do you need to learn? What do you need to change? What small steps must you take today? Figure that out, then just do it. Truly live in the present, and you'll lay a positive foundation for the future.*

"Faith keeps the person that keeps the faith."

—Mother Teresa

■ *Always focus your vision beyond your own circumstances and look to God for direction. He will never lead you astray, and He will never let you down.*

"Anyone who takes hope away from the young is a murderer. It is a sin to impart your own disillusionments, to share your disappointments and to rob them of an openness to life which is the chief blessing of the young."

—Charlie Chaplin

■ *Protect your hope. Nurture it. Never allow those who have lost their own hope to steal yours.*

"There are no hopeless situations; there are only men who have grown hopeless about them."

—Motto of Marshall Ferdinand Foch,
the Hero of Verdun

■ *If things look bleak, clear away the clouds within your mind. If the sun shines there, the rest of the world looks bright.*

"Finish each day and be done with it . . . you have done what you could; some blunders and absurdities no doubt crept in; forget them as soon as you can. Tomorrow is a new day; you shall begin it well and serenely."

—Ralph Waldo Emerson

■ *Right before you go to sleep tonight, learn what you can from your mistakes and then forget about them. Don't carry yesterday's baggage with you into the future. Start each day fresh. Approach it as if it's going to be the best day of your life.*

"Hope is the foundation of all change."

—Author Unknown

■ *As long as you believe that you can make an impact on your world, you have the potential to make it happen.*

"Encouragement is the fuel for tomorrow."

—Author Unknown

■ *Give the gift of encouragement to others. Reward them for today, and give them hope for tomorrow. A person can travel farther on a kind word than on just about anything else in life.*

"The best thing about the future is that it comes only one day at a time."

—Abraham Lincoln

■ *Don't allow the future to intimidate you. Meet each day with the best you have.*

"The best way to predict the future is to make it happen."

—Alan Kay, Executive,
Apple Computers

■ *The things you do today are an investment for tomorrow. The greater the price you are paying, the greater the potential dividends you may receive. If you want to know what your future will look like, find its pattern in the present.*

"God can do anything, but He won't until He can do it through a person. Faith is limited only by us."

—Author Unknown

■ *For some reason God intends to fulfill His plan on earth by using people. Why He has chosen to do it that way is one of life's great mysteries. But of one thing we can be certain: Whatever it is that's not getting done right now is because of us, not Him.*

"The pace of events is moving so fast that unless we can find some way to keep our sights on tomorrow, we cannot expect to be in touch with today."

—Dean Rusk,
Former U.S. Secretary of State

■ *The only way to be prepared for an ever-changing tomorrow is to keep growing and changing yourself today.*

"We cannot rewrite the past, but we can write the future."

—Author Unknown

■ *What kind of story is your life going to be? A tragedy? A comedy? A tale of great adventure? No matter what's been written up to today, you can always change the direction of the story. Is it time in your life for a plot twist?*

"God will not suffer man to have a knowledge of things to come; for if he had prescience of his prosperity, he would be careless; and if understanding of his adversity, he would be despairing and senseless."

—St. Augustine

■ *Don't wait for God to show you your future to start living your life. He'll show you what you need to know. Instead, ask God how you can be obedient to Him today, and He'll take care of the rest.*

"Today's world cannot be remodeled with yesterday's memories: There are no u-turns on the road to the future."

—Michael O'Neill, Journalist

■ *Plan for the future, live in the present, and leave yesterday behind.*

"We have too many men of science and too few men of God. We have grasped the mystery of the atom, and rejected the Sermon on the Mount. The world has achieved brilliance without wisdom, power without conscience. Ours is a world of nuclear giants and ethical infants. We know more about war than we know about peace, more about killing than we know about living."

—General Omar Bradley

■ *Everything in life changes. Scientific theories come and go; styles and fashions change with the seasons; technology marches on. Put your faith in the One who will never leave you behind or pass you by: God. He will never fail you.*

"God will allow His servant to succeed when he has learned that success does not make him dearer to God nor more valuable in the total scheme of things."

—A. W. Tozer

■ *No matter what you do, God will never love you more (or less) than He does at this moment. We cannot earn His love. It is a gift. Only once we receive it can we truly live as He intends us to.*

"Until you believe in yourself, you won't believe in your future."

—Author Unknown

■ *Belief in yourself isn't ego or arrogance. It's knowing who you are and believing—despite your flaws—that God can and will use you for something significant in His plan.*

"Every man, woman, and child I've ever met, seen, or heard wants one thing more than anything else in the world: tomorrow."

—John Wayne

■ Tomorrow. *The word has a nice ring to it. The hope of a better future is what keeps many people going. Spend your life in such a way that you and others get to live that better tomorrow.*

"Think a dynamic future—work in a dynamic present. We should all be concerned about the future because we will have to spend the rest of our lives there."

—Charles F. Kettering

■ *Remember that your future is not set in stone. It is being created today.*

"Whatever you do today, do it better tomorrow."

—Robert Schuller

■ *Don't let a day go by that you don't try to improve yourself in some way. Spend time with great men and women of vision. Improve your mind with books, articles, and tapes. Leave your comfort zone. Pay the price to reach your potential.*

"When we walk to the edge of all the light we have, and take that step into the darkness of the unknown, we must believe that one of two things will happen—there will be something solid for us to stand on, or we will be taught to fly."

—*Christian Medical Society Journal,*
Vol. XVI, No. 2, 1985

■ *Never let another person tell you that something cannot be done. God may have been waiting centuries for you to come along so that you could do the impossible for Him.*

"Nothing worth doing is completed in our lifetime; therefore, we must be saved by hope."

—Reinhold Niebuhr

■ *When everything is said and done, only that which is eternal is worthy of your life.*

ABOUT THE
AUTHOR

Dr. John C. Maxwell is one of the top thinkers and equippers in the United States today in the area of personal and corporate leadership development. A dynamic motivational communicator, he speaks to more than 150,000 people each year and is in great demand nationally and internationally on topics such as leadership, personal growth, attitude, relationship building, and Christian living.

He has spoken to such diverse organizations as Chick-fil-a, Amway, the Salvation Army, Creative Marketing, The Christian Booksellers Association, the National Collegiate Athletic Association, the Salem Communications Corporation, Home Interiors, and several professional sports teams. He frequently teams with other notable business and personal growth experts.

John has more than twenty-five years of experience in organizational leadership and holds an earned doctorate as well as two honorary ones. He is the author of more than a dozen books with more than half a million copies in print. His titles include, *The Success Journey, Developing the Leader Within You, Developing the Leaders Around You, Breakthrough Parenting,* and *The Winning Attitude.*

Additional Leadership, Personal Growth, and Church Growth Resources Developed by John C. Maxwell Are Available from INJOY (800) 333-6506

INJOY is a Christian leadership organization dedicated to helping leaders reach their potential in ministry, business, and the family.

Through INJOY, John Maxwell offers a wide range of training seminars, books, videos, and audiocassette programs designed to increase an individual's ability to influence and lead others.

A unique resource is the INJOY Life Club, a one-hour equipping tape for pastors and Christian leaders taught by John Maxwell. It is currently mailed each month to more than 10,000 subscribers, and that number is growing rapidly.

Another exciting resource offered by John Maxwell each month is "Maximum Impact," a leadership equipping tape for the businessperson working in the marketplace. It's like having a professional business seminar come to you every month!

To receive a catalog of resources available from INJOY or additional information regarding

John Maxwell's speaking itinerary or
motivational materials, please contact INJOY at:

(800) 333-6506
http://www.injoy.com

Let John Maxwell take you to the next level!

John Maxwell has spent more than a quarter of a century helping people reach their potential. And he wants to do the same for you.

To become all you can be, read these insightful and motivating books by John Maxwell:

The Success Journey

In a refreshingly straightforward and humorous style, Maxwell shares unique insights into what it means to be successful. And he reveals a definition that puts genuine success within your reach yet motivates you to keep striving for your dreams.

Developing the Leader Within You

Being a leader means more than having a position or title. True leadership is influence. Learn to lead from one of the nation's top experts. This book is a must for anyone in management, business, or any leadership position.

Developing the Leaders Around You

Great leaders are never content to lead followers. They develop and lead other leaders. Receive inspired instruction on mentoring and team building from this gifted motivator.

The Winning Attitude

Most people are very close to becoming the person God wants them to be. What enables them to take the next step? The right attitude! Let John show you how to be a winner.

Published by Thomas Nelson Publishers.
Available in bookstores.